MW01169896

GROWTH MINDSET

LIFE SKILLS FOR KIDS

Inspiring Stories to Build Resilience, Self-Esteem, and Confidence

EMILY LYLANI

TABLE OF CONTENTS

INTRODUCTION

What do you do when you're faced with a challenge? Do you roll up your sleeves and say, "Bring it on!" or do you sometimes think, "I'm not sure I can do this"? What if I told you there's a superpower that can help you tackle any challenge, no matter how big or small? It's not something from a comic book or a movie—this superpower is something that lives inside your brain, and it's called a growth mindset.

Have you ever heard someone say, "I'm just not good at this" or "I'll never get better"? That's called a fixed mindset—thinking that you're stuck with the abilities you have right now and can't improve. But what if, instead of thinking that, you could say, "I can learn this with some effort" or "Mistakes are just part of getting better"? That's a growth mindset, and it's like hitting the "power-up" button in your brain! It's all about believing you can grow and get better with practice, hard work, and a little patience.

Which sounds more fun—being stuck or knowing you can always improve?

Have you ever felt nervous before a test, a game, or trying something new? That's where confidence steps in—it helps you believe in yourself, even when things seem tricky. Do you ever compare yourself to others and feel like you're not good enough? That's when self-esteem reminds you that you're awesome just as you are, no matter what anyone else thinks. And what about when something doesn't go your way—do you keep trying or give up? That's where resilience kicks in, helping you bounce back from mistakes or tough situations stronger than before.

These three traits—confidence, self-esteem, and resilience—are the keys to unlocking a growth mindset. They help you tackle challenges, pick yourself up when things don't go perfectly, and keep moving forward.

Ever wonder how some of the most amazing people in history got where they are? They weren't born with all the answers or with everything figured out. In fact, many of them struggled at first—just like we all do! But here's the cool part: they used a growth mindset to push through those struggles. Whether it's Thomas Edison failing over a thousand times to invent the light bulb or Malala Yousafzai standing up for what she believed in, these real-life heroes show us that challenges are just stepping stones to success.

This book is packed with their stories— stories of people who didn't give up, who believed in themselves, and who found strength in every setback. And guess what? You can do the same.

Are you ready to discover your superpower? Let's jump into the stories of these incredible people and see how you can use their lessons to boost your confidence, build your self-esteem, and grow your resilience. Your adventure starts now!

PART ONE

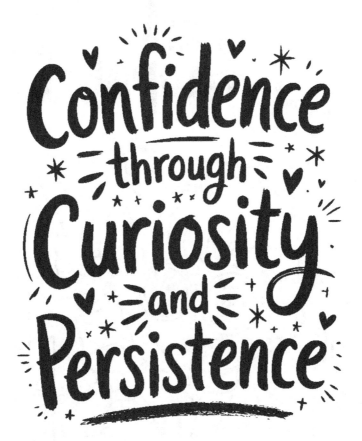

CHAPTER 1:

Thomas Edison – The Power of Persistence

Let me introduce you to a guy named Thomas Edison. You probably know him as the inventor of the light bulb, but did you know that his journey to that bright idea was full of mistakes and failures? In fact, it took him over 10,000 tries to get it right. Sounds pretty wild, right? Well, let's dive into his story and see what made him so amazing.

Back in the 1800s, people didn't have light bulbs like we do today. When it got dark outside, they lit their homes with candles or gas lamps, which weren't always bright or safe. Edison had a big idea—what if he could invent a bulb that could light up without a flame, last a long time, and be safe to use? He was determined to make it happen.

But here's the thing—Edison didn't know how to make a light bulb. There was no "how-to" guide for inventing something like that. So he started experimenting, trying to figure out which materials could glow without burning out too quickly. His first thought was to use different types of metal wires inside the glass bulb. He tried platinum, and it heated up but didn't last very long. He tried copper, but that fizzled out even faster. Then he tested things like cotton thread and even hair—none of them worked.

But did Edison stop? Not even close! Every time something failed, he learned something new. And instead of feeling frustrated, he got curious. "What else can I try?" he asked himself. Sometimes, his workshop looked like a giant science experiment gone wrong—

wires, bulbs, and materials scattered everywhere. His team thought he was kind of crazy, but Edison kept smiling through the mess. He believed every failure was just one step closer to success.

Edison's friends and fellow inventors started to doubt him. Some even told him, "Maybe you should give up, Tom. This light bulb thing isn't going to work." But Edison wasn't the kind of person to quit just because things got tough. He had a special superpower—persistence. That means he didn't give up, no matter how many times something didn't work.

Then, one day, after years of trial and error, Edison discovered something special: carbonized bamboo. This material lasted longer than anything else he had tried. When Edison put it inside his bulb, it glowed bright and steady. It didn't fizzle out like the other materials. He had finally found the perfect solution! After more than 10,000 experiments, Thomas Edison invented the first practical light bulb.

Think about that—10,000 tries! That's like failing at something every day for nearly 30 years. But instead of feeling discouraged, Edison believed he was getting closer with each attempt. He once said, "I have not failed. I've just found 10,000 ways that won't work." It was this persistence that lit up the world. Thanks to Edison's invention, we can now read at night, light up our homes, and keep our streets bright after sunset.

So, what can we learn from Edison's story? It shows us that even if something feels impossible, even if people tell you to stop, you should never give up on your ideas. Sometimes, the road to success is long and filled with mistakes, but every failure is just a step toward something incredible. Just imagine if Edison had quit after 9,999 tries—our world might still be in the dark!

So, when you have an idea, hold onto it. Even if it doesn't work right away, keep going. Who knows what amazing things you'll discover when you refuse to give up, just like Thomas Edison did with his light bulb!

CHAPTER 2:

Marie Curie – Breaking Boundaries

Let's step into the world of Marie Curie, a woman who didn't just break the rules—she shattered them. Imagine living in a time when women weren't supposed to be scientists or even think about working in labs. Most people believed science was a job for men and women were better off staying home. But Marie? She didn't care about those silly rules. She knew she was destined to make incredible discoveries, and no one was going to stop her.

Marie was born in Poland in 1867, a time when girls weren't allowed to go to university. But Marie loved learning. She was curious about the world and especially fascinated by science—how the universe worked, what everything was made of, and how tiny particles behaved in ways we couldn't see. So, when Marie was old enough, she packed her bags and moved to Paris to study at the Sorbonne, one of the best universities in the world. Even though she had to leave her family and her country behind, Marie was determined to follow her passion.

When she arrived at the university, things weren't exactly easy. Marie was often the only woman in her classes, surrounded by men who didn't believe she could keep up. But instead of feeling scared or out of place, Marie felt confident. She knew she belonged there. Every time someone doubted her, she worked even harder, studying late into the night. Soon, Marie wasn't just keeping up with her classmates—she was outshining them. Her professors were amazed by her talent and dedication.

Marie's passion for science led her to an incredible discovery—something that would change the world forever. Working alongside her husband, Pierre, Marie studied mysterious elements that gave off energy on their own. She called this energy radioactivity, a word she invented herself! Through her experiments, Marie discovered two new elements—polonium and radium—that emitted this strange, invisible energy. She realized these radioactive materials could be used in medicine to help people and in other ways, no one had imagined before.

But Marie's journey wasn't easy. The world of science was still dominated by men, and many people thought her discoveries were just lucky guesses or Pierre's ideas. When she won her first Nobel Prize—the highest award a scientist can get—many believed it was her husband who deserved the credit. But Marie knew the truth. She had worked just as hard, if not harder, to make those discoveries. And she didn't stop there. She went on to win a second Nobel Prize, making her the first person ever to win two!

Marie's story teaches us something really important: confidence grows when you follow your passion. Even when the world tells you "no," when people say you can't do something, or when the path seems tough, believing in yourself and your dreams is what makes all the difference. Marie didn't let anyone else decide her future—she took charge, and her discoveries changed science forever.

Imagine if Marie had listened to the people who told her she wasn't good enough. What if she had stayed home instead of going to Paris? What if she had given up after the first person said, "Women can't do science"? We wouldn't know about radioactivity, and many important medical treatments might not exist today. But Marie followed her heart, and that's why we remember her as one of the greatest scientists who ever lived.

So, whenever you feel unsure or wonder if you should follow your passion, think of Marie Curie. Confidence doesn't come from being perfect or always knowing the answers. It comes from chasing what you love, even when the odds are against you. Who knows what you'll discover if you follow your own path, just like Marie did?

CHAPTER 3:

Leonardo da Vinci – Embracing Curiosity

Have you ever looked up at the stars and wondered how far away they really are? Or watched a bird soaring through the sky and thought, "How do they stay up there without falling?" These big questions filled the mind of Leonardo da Vinci, a curious genius who lived over 500 years ago. Leonardo was more than just a brilliant painter—he was an inventor, a scientist, and a dreamer. He believed that being curious could unlock the secrets of the universe, and his life was a wild adventure of discovery!

Leonardo was born in 1452 in a tiny village in Italy. As a kid, he didn't have fancy schools or computers. Instead, he had something even better: a big imagination and a love for exploring the world around him! While other kids played games, Leonardo was busy observing nature. He would spend hours watching birds flapping their wings, studying how water flowed in rivers, and sketching everything he saw. He was on a quest to understand how everything worked, and he never stopped asking questions.

When he turned 14, Leonardo became an apprentice to a famous painter in Florence named Andrea del Verrocchio. Imagine this: he was learning to paint, sculpt, and create amazing artwork in a bustling city filled with creativity! But Leonardo wasn't satisfied with just being good at art; he wanted to understand the science behind it. He studied how light and shadow played on objects and how human muscles moved. He even had the courage to dissect dead bodies (yikes!) to learn about the human body's secrets. Talk about dedication!

One of Leonardo's most famous masterpieces is the Mona Lisa, but it's not just her mysterious smile that makes her special. Leonardo spent years perfecting his techniques, using layers of paint to create soft edges and a lifelike appearance. It's like he breathed life into the canvas! People have admired the Mona Lisa for centuries, and her smile still leaves everyone guessing. What is she thinking? Thanks to Leonardo's endless curiosity about how people express emotions, we get to enjoy her captivating gaze.

But hold on, that's not all! Leonardo's imagination soared beyond painting. He dreamed about flying. Yes, flying! He was fascinated by birds, especially how they soared gracefully through the air. He sketched designs for flying machines—some that look just like our modern-day helicopters! Although he didn't have the technology to build them, his ideas planted the seeds for future inventors. Can you imagine being the first person to think about flying?

Now, let's talk about his notebooks. Oh boy, these are treasure chests of ideas! Leonardo wrote everything down in his notebooks, filling them with sketches of flying machines, scuba gear, and even armored tanks—yes, he imagined tanks before they were even invented! His notebook pages were alive with his wild ideas, and they were written in a funny way called mirror writing. He wrote backward, making it tricky for anyone else to read. Maybe he did this to keep his secrets safe, or maybe he just liked being different!

Leonardo wasn't just an artist; he was a scientist at heart. He studied how water moved, the shapes of clouds, and the way plants grew. He believed that understanding nature was key to inventing better machines. His investigations into hydraulics led him to create designs for water pumps and irrigation systems, helping farmers and cities thrive. Imagine him in a muddy field, sketching his ideas while the water splashed around!

So, what's the big lesson we can learn from Leonardo da Vinci? It's simple: curiosity leads to mastery in many fields. Leonardo was never afraid to ask questions, explore the unknown, and follow his interests, no matter how unusual they seemed. Whether he was painting the world's most famous portrait or dreaming up fantastical inventions, his curious mind was always at work.

Whenever you find yourself wondering about how something works or why things happen, remember Leonardo! Don't just let those questions float away like balloons in the sky—grab hold of them! Dive into your curiosity and see where it takes you. Just like Leonardo, your questions could lead to incredible discoveries and maybe even change the world!

I believe in my dreams.

CHAPTER 4:

J.K. Rowling - From Rejection to Global Success

Imagine a world where magic is real, where wands wave, spells are cast, and fantastic creatures roam the land. Sounds like a dream, right? Well, it was J.K. Rowling who turned that dream into reality with her incredible Harry Potter series! But before she became one of the most famous authors in the world, Rowling faced a mountain of challenges that would make anyone want to throw in the towel. Instead, she chose to believe in her vision, and that changed everything!

Once upon a time in the cozy town of Edinburgh, Scotland, there lived a young girl named Joanne. From a very early age, Joanne loved to read and write. She would spend hours lost in her imagination, dreaming up magical lands and extraordinary adventures. But as she grew older, life wasn't always easy. After finishing school, she faced some tough times. She struggled to find work, and there were days when she had little money to spare. But through it all, she never stopped writing. In fact, she had a wild idea brewing in her mind—a story about a young boy who didn't know he was a wizard!

On a train ride from Manchester to London, the idea of Harry Potter popped into Joanne's head like a brilliant spark. She imagined Harry's journey to Hogwarts School of Witchcraft and Wizardry, complete with magical classes, exciting friends, and, of course, a very mysterious dark wizard named Voldemort. It was an idea that made her heart race with excitement! But when she started writing, it wasn't all smooth sailing.

After she finished her first draft of the book, Joanne was bursting with hope. She believed in her story and wanted to share it with the world. But guess what? The first publishers she approached didn't see the magic in her words. They rejected her manuscript over and over again! Can you imagine pouring your heart and soul into something, only to have people tell you "no"? It was disheartening, and many people would have given up. But not Joanne! She knew deep down that her story was special, and she wasn't going to let anyone take that away from her.

After facing twelve rejections, a small publisher called Bloomsbury finally decided to give her a chance. They believed in her vision and agreed to publish the first book, Harry Potter and the Philosopher's Stone (or Harry Potter and the Sorcerer's Stone if you're in the U.S.). But even then, things didn't magically change overnight. The publisher only printed a small number of copies, and it wasn't until a few lucky kids got their hands on the book that word began to spread like wildfire!

Soon, children everywhere were captivated by Harry's world of spells, potions, and friendship. The books flew off the shelves, and Rowling found herself facing a new challenge: how to manage her newfound fame! Her perseverance had paid off, and Harry Potter became a global phenomenon, making Rowling one of the most beloved authors of all time.

But even with all the success, Rowling never forgot how hard she worked to get there. She often said that confidence comes from believing in your vision, even when things seem impossible. She encourages kids everywhere to never give up on their dreams, no matter how many "no's" they might face.

So, what's the biggest lesson we can learn from J.K. Rowling? It's that confidence comes from believing in your vision. Even when the world was telling her "no," she held tight to her dreams and didn't let rejection define her. Whenever you feel discouraged or think about giving up, remember Rowling's story. Whether it's writing a book, playing a sport, or learning a new skill, believe in yourself and your ideas. You never know— your magic might be just around the corner!

With Harry Potter, Rowling opened the door to a world where anyone can find their magic. Who knows? Maybe your own amazing story is waiting to be written. All you have to do is believe in yourself and keep dreaming big!

CHAPTER 5:

Walt Disney – Creating Magic from Imagination

Do you believe in magic? If you've ever watched a Disney movie, visited a Disney park, or met Mickey Mouse, you probably do! But did you know that the man behind all that magic, Walt Disney, didn't always have it easy? His journey was filled with ups and downs, but his incredible imagination and unwavering confidence helped him create a world that brings joy to millions. Let's dive into his story!

Once upon a time, in a little town in Illinois, a boy named Walt grew up with a wild imagination. From a young age, he loved to draw and create stories. While other kids were playing outside, Walt would be busy sketching animals and dreaming up fantastic adventures. He was enchanted by the world of animation and wanted to make his own cartoons. But it wasn't all fun and games for young Walt!

After finishing school, Walt wanted to break into the world of animation. He worked hard, but guess what? His first attempt at starting a company called Laugh-O-Gram Studios didn't go quite as planned. It turned out to be a flop! Instead of bringing laughter, it brought him heartache when the company went bankrupt. Many people would have thrown in the towel after such a tough blow, but not Walt! He believed that failure was just a stepping stone to success.

After that setback, Walt packed his bags and moved to Hollywood, where he hoped to make his big dreams come true. But his journey still had more bumps ahead. Can you believe that he was actually fired from a newspaper job for "lacking imagination"? Imagine that! The very thing he loved most was being dismissed! But rather than let it get him down, Walt dusted himself off and kept dreaming.

Walt eventually teamed up with his brother Roy, and together they founded the Disney Brothers Studio. With sheer determination, they began creating short cartoons, and one of their early characters, Oswald the Lucky Rabbit, became a hit! But wait! Just when things were looking up, Walt lost the rights to Oswald. It was another crushing blow, but instead of giving up, he channeled his frustration into something even bigger—he created a new character, Mickey Mouse!

With Mickey, Walt found his voice and brought his imagination to life. Mickey's first big appearance was in a silent cartoon called Plane Crazy, but it was the famous Steamboat Willie that truly captured everyone's heart. People loved Mickey's cheerful spirit and adventurous personality! From that moment on, Walt knew he was onto something magical.

But Walt's imagination didn't stop there! He dreamed of creating entire worlds filled with rides, attractions, and beloved characters. In 1955, his dream came true with the opening of Disneyland in California. Imagine walking into a place where fairy tales come to life, where you can meet princesses and fly through the stars on thrilling rides! Walt's vision transformed the amusement park experience forever, and Disneyland became a place where families create unforgettable memories.

So, what can we learn from Walt Disney? It's clear: confidence in your imagination can change the world! Despite countless setbacks and rejections, Walt never lost faith in his dreams. He showed us that imagination is a powerful tool. When you believe in your ideas and dare to think outside the box, you can create something truly magical.

Whenever you find yourself dreaming big or facing challenges, remember Walt's journey. Whether you want to draw, write, invent, or even start your own company, let your imagination soar! Who knows? Your dreams might change the world, just like Walt Disney did!

PART TWO

SELF-ESTEEM THROUGH SELF-BELIEF

CHAPTER 6:

Albert Einstein – Redefining Intelligence

Do you ever feel like you don't quite fit in at school? Maybe you struggle with certain subjects while your friends seem to breeze through them. Well, let me introduce you to a guy who totally shook things up in the world of science! His name is Albert Einstein, and he's one of the most famous scientists in history. But guess what? He wasn't always the star student everyone expected him to be!

Born in a little town in Germany, Albert was a curious kid who loved to ask questions. While other children played outside, he often found himself lost in thought, pondering the mysteries of the universe. Why does the sky turn blue? What makes things move? These questions fascinated him! But when he entered school, things took a turn for the worse.

You see, Albert didn't quite fit the mold of what his teachers wanted him to be. He found traditional schooling boring and rigid. Instead of memorizing facts and figures, he wanted to explore ideas and think creatively. Can you imagine sitting in class while everyone else is focused, and you're dreaming about the secrets of the stars? His teachers thought he was lazy and not very bright because he struggled to follow their rules. They didn't understand his way of thinking, and that hurt.

Even though he faced challenges in school, Albert never stopped believing in himself. He knew he was smart in his own unique way! After finishing school, he had a hard time finding a job. Imagine being a brilliant mind and struggling to get a foot in the door! But instead of giving up, Albert kept working hard. He found a job at a patent office, where he could think about his ideas during the day and work on his scientific theories in his spare time.

Then came the moment that changed everything! In 1905, while working at the patent office, he published four groundbreaking papers that would change the world of physics forever. One of those papers introduced his famous theory of relativity, which explained how time and space are intertwined. Whoa! That's some serious brainpower! People finally started to notice Albert's genius, and he quickly became one of the most important scientists of all time.

His work revolutionized our understanding of the universe and even led to the development of technologies we use today, like GPS! And all this from a boy who didn't fit in at school! Albert's journey shows us that self-belief allows you to define success on your terms. He didn't let others' opinions shape how he saw himself. Instead, he embraced his unique perspective and followed his passion for discovery.

So, if you ever feel different or struggle with school, remember Albert Einstein. Your path might not look like everyone else's, but that's what makes it special! Keep asking questions, stay curious, and believe in your own brilliance. You have the power to redefine what success means for you, just like Albert did!

When you embrace who you are and chase your dreams, there's no telling how far you can go. So go ahead—let your imagination soar, just like Einstein did, and maybe one day, you'll change the world, too!

CHAPTER 7:

Frida Kahlo – Turning Pain into Art

Have you ever felt like the world sees you differently than you see yourself? Or maybe you've faced challenges that made you feel like giving up. Well, let me introduce you to an incredible artist who turned her struggles into stunning masterpieces! Her name is Frida Kahlo, and her story is as colorful and vibrant as her paintings.

Frida was born in Coyoacán, Mexico, in 1907. From a young age, she was a dreamer, often doodling and painting as a way to express herself. But life had its ups and downs, and when Frida was just 18 years old, she faced a life-changing accident. While riding a bus, a terrible crash occurred, and Frida was seriously injured. It was a tough time for her; she had to endure many surgeries and long periods of recovery. Imagine being in so much pain and feeling trapped inside your own body!

But here's where Frida's spirit shined brightly. Instead of letting her pain defeat her, she turned it into something beautiful. During her recovery, she began to paint. She created a canvas that reflected not just her struggles but her soul. Her artwork was unlike anything anyone had seen before—bold colors, powerful symbols, and deep emotions filled every piece. Frida poured her heart into her paintings, using them to express her pain, identity, and the experiences that shaped her.

One of her most famous paintings is called "The Two Fridas." In it, she portrays two versions of herself: one is dressed in traditional Mexican clothing, while the other is in a European-style dress. This painting represents her mixed heritage and the duality of her identity. Frida's art was a way for her to explore who she was and to share her story with the world.

Frida's unique style and perspective made her stand out in the art world. She became a symbol of strength and resilience, inspiring countless people with her ability to transform suffering into creativity. Through her art, she showed that our experiences, both good and bad, shape who we are.

So, what can we learn from Frida Kahlo? Self-esteem grows by embracing your uniqueness. She celebrated her individuality, even when the world tried to define her by her pain. Instead of hiding her scars, she showcased them in her art, reminding us that everyone has a story to tell.

If you ever feel different or face challenges, remember Frida's journey. Embrace your uniqueness and let it shine! Your experiences make you who you are, and that's something to celebrate. Whether it's through art, writing, or any other form of expression, don't be afraid to share your story.

So, go ahead! Grab a paintbrush, a pen, or even a guitar, and let your creativity flow. You have the power to turn your pain into something beautiful, just like Frida did. Remember, the world needs your voice, and it's time to let it be heard!

CHAPTER 8:

Malala Yousafzai – Fighting for Education

Do you believe in the power of education? What if I told you that one brave girl fought for the right to go to school, even when it was dangerous? Meet Malala Yousafzai, a true superhero in the fight for education! Her story is a shining example of courage and determination that shows us how powerful one voice can be.

Malala was born in Pakistan in 1997, in a beautiful valley called Swat. Growing up, she loved learning and dreamed of becoming a doctor. Her father, who was a school principal, encouraged her curiosity and helped her realize how important education is. But not everyone felt the same way. In her hometown, a group called the Taliban had taken control, and they didn't believe that girls should go to school. Imagine being told that your dreams were impossible just because of who you are!

But Malala wasn't about to let anyone silence her. She felt strongly that every girl, including herself, deserved an education. So, she decided to speak out! She began writing a blog under a fake name, sharing her thoughts about the importance of education and the challenges girls faced. Through her words, she inspired many people to join her cause. Malala's bravery shone bright, and soon, she became a voice for millions of girls who wanted to learn.

However, standing up for what is right can be dangerous. In 2012, when Malala was just 15 years old, she was attacked by the Taliban while riding home from school. It was a scary moment that could have stopped anyone in their tracks. But guess what? Malala didn't back down. She survived and became even more determined to fight for education. Her courage inspired people all around the world, and she soon became a global symbol of hope.

In 2014, Malala achieved something extraordinary—she became the youngest-ever recipient of the Nobel Peace Prize! Can you imagine that? At just 17 years old, she was recognized for her fearless fight for girls' education. Malala didn't just stop there; she continued to advocate for education through her organization, the Malala Fund, which helps girls go to school in countries where education is still under threat.

So, what can we learn from Malala Yousafzai? Self-esteem comes from standing up for what's right. She showed us that even when the odds are stacked against you, your voice can make a difference. It takes courage to stand up for what you believe in, but when you do, you inspire others to join you.

Whenever you see someone being treated unfairly, or if you feel passionate about something important, remember Malala's incredible journey. You have the power to make a change, no matter how small you think it is. Whether it's standing up for your friends, helping others, or even just sharing your ideas, your voice matters!

So, go ahead! Be brave, be bold, and stand up for what you believe in. Like Malala, you can change the world one step at a time!

CHAPTER 9:

Stephen Hawking – Defying Physical Limitations

Have you ever looked up at the stars and wondered what's out there? Or have you thought about how the universe works? If you have, you're in great company! Let me introduce you to an amazing man who not only wondered about the universe but also helped us understand it better. His name is Stephen Hawking, and his story is a fantastic example of how determination can shine bright, even in the face of tough challenges!

Stephen was born in Oxford, England, in 1942. From a young age, he was curious about everything—stars, planets, and the mysteries of the universe. He loved to explore science and would often ask questions that made his teachers scratch their heads in amazement. But just as he was setting out on his exciting journey as a physicist, something unexpected happened.

When Stephen was just 21 years old, he received some tough news. Doctors diagnosed him with ALS (Amyotrophic Lateral Sclerosis), a condition that affects the muscles and makes it harder to move. Imagine being told that your body would change in ways you couldn't control! Many people might have given up, but not Stephen. He decided to focus on what he could do instead of what he couldn't.

Despite his physical challenges, Stephen never stopped dreaming big! He went on to study at the prestigious Cambridge

University and became a world-renowned physicist. Using a special computer system that allowed him to communicate, Stephen shared his brilliant ideas about black holes and the nature of the universe. He even wrote a best-selling book called "A Brief History of Time" that explained complex ideas about space and time in a way everyone could understand. Imagine writing a book that millions of people read, all while dealing with a serious illness!

Stephen's work changed the way we think about the universe. He showed that black holes can actually give off radiation, which was a groundbreaking discovery! He made physics exciting and accessible for everyone, and his spirit inspired many people around the world.

So, what can we learn from Stephen Hawking? Self-esteem stems from focusing on what you can achieve, not your limitations. He showed us that it's not about what you

can't do; it's about what you can do!
Stephen's story teaches us that we all have
unique talents and abilities, and it's
important to nurture them, no matter what
challenges we face.

When you feel like giving up or think
something is too hard, remember Stephen's
incredible journey. He didn't let his illness
define him; instead, he focused on exploring
the stars and sharing his love of science with
the world. Whether it's art, sports, science,
or anything else you're passionate about,
embrace it with all your heart!

So, dream big, reach for the stars, and never
let anything hold you back. Like Stephen, you
have the power to make amazing things
happen, no matter the obstacles you face.
Remember, your potential is limitless—just
like the universe!

CHAPTER 10:

Serena Williams – Mental Strength of a Champion

Imagine standing on a bright green tennis court, the sun shining down, and the sound of a ball being struck echoing in the air. Now, picture a powerful player running back and forth, swinging her racket with fierce determination. That player is Serena Williams, and she is known for more than just her incredible skills; she's famous for her unstoppable mindset!

Born in Saginaw, Michigan, in 1981, Serena started playing tennis at a very young age, often practicing alongside her sister Venus. While most kids were playing video games or riding bikes, Serena was out on the court, dreaming of becoming a champion. But her journey was anything but easy. She faced many hurdles, including tough opponents and people who doubted her talent. Did she let that stop her? No way!

Serena knew that to succeed, she had to be mentally tough. It wasn't enough to just be a great player; she needed to believe in herself, especially during the most challenging moments. When she found herself down in a match, instead of panicking, she practiced focusing her thoughts. She would take deep breaths, visualize herself winning the point, and remind herself of all the hard work she had put in. Imagine being in the middle of a nail-biting match and feeling calm and ready! That's the magic of having a strong mindset.

In 1999, after years of hard work and dedication, Serena won her first Grand Slam title at the U.S. Open, and she was just getting started! Over the years, she racked up an astonishing 23 Grand Slam singles titles, becoming one of the most celebrated athletes in history. Her journey didn't just break records; it shattered expectations and inspired countless young people, especially girls, to dream big and believe they could achieve anything.

So, what can we learn from the incredible Serena Williams? Confidence comes from mastering your mindset. She taught us that while talent is important, it's our attitude and determination that truly set us apart. When challenges come knocking, it's your confidence and mental strength that will help you overcome them.

When you face a tough task—be it a tricky homework assignment, a big game, or trying something new—think about Serena's inspiring story. She didn't let obstacles stop her; instead, she transformed them into stepping stones on her path to success.

Embrace your inner Serena! Take a deep breath, visualize your victory, and tackle those challenges with courage. Like Serena, you have the power to be a champion in your own life. Your mindset is a powerful tool—wield it wisely, and you can achieve amazing things!

PART THREE

Resilience in the Face of Adversity

CHAPTER 11:

Nelson Mandela – The Strength of Forgiveness

What would you do if you were locked away for years and years, all because you stood up for what you believed in? That's exactly what Nelson Mandela faced! His story is a powerful reminder of the strength of forgiveness and the amazing resilience of the human spirit.

Nelson was born in Transkei, South Africa, in 1918. From a young age, he dreamed of a world where everyone, regardless of their skin color, could live together peacefully.

However, during Nelson's childhood, South Africa was divided by a terrible system called apartheid. This meant that people of different races were treated unfairly and unequally. Nelson couldn't stand to see his friends and family suffer, so he decided to take action. He became a leader in the fight against apartheid, believing that change was possible.

However, fighting for justice didn't come without consequences. In 1962, Nelson was arrested for his activism and sentenced to 27 years in prison! Can you imagine spending nearly three decades locked away? During his time in prison on Robben Island, he faced harsh conditions, working in the hot sun and living in a tiny cell. But even in those dark times, Nelson held onto hope. He refused to let his spirit be broken. Instead of harboring anger or seeking revenge, he focused on his vision of a united South Africa.

After his release in 1990, Nelson became a symbol of peace and reconciliation. He didn't seek revenge against those who had wronged him; instead, he chose forgiveness. This is where his incredible strength shone! He believed that holding onto anger would only hurt himself and others. By forgiving his oppressors, he showed the world that true resilience comes from embracing love and understanding, even after enduring great hardship.

In 1994, after years of struggle, Nelson Mandela became South Africa's first black president and worked tirelessly to heal his country. He brought people together and inspired millions to believe in a brighter future. His message was simple but powerful: Resilience is shown through forgiveness and enduring hardship.

So, what can we learn from Nelson Mandela?

When faced with challenges or conflict, instead of letting anger and bitterness take over, we can choose to rise above it. Just like Mandela, we can show strength by forgiving others and focusing on building a better tomorrow.

Whenever you feel upset or wronged, remember Nelson's story. Embracing forgiveness can free your heart and mind, allowing you to move forward with hope and strength. You have the power to change the world around you, one act of kindness at a time!

CHAPTER 12:

Helen Keller - Overcoming the Impossible

Some stories shine brighter than others, and the story of Helen Keller is one of those shining tales! Helen faced challenges that would make most people want to give up, but instead, she chose to embrace her circumstances and inspire the world.

Born in Tuscumbia, Alabama, in 1880, Helen was a lively and curious child. However, her life took a dramatic turn when she was just 19 months old. A sudden illness left her both blind and deaf, plunging her into a dark and silent world. It was like being in a room filled with shadows, unable to see or hear anyone around her. Despite her difficulties, Helen's spirit remained unbroken.

Then, a remarkable woman named Anne Sullivan entered her life. Anne was like a magical key that could unlock Helen's potential. With incredible patience and love, she began teaching Helen how to communicate, using touch as their connection. It wasn't always easy. There were moments of frustration when Helen felt trapped in her own mind, unable to express her thoughts and feelings. But Anne never gave up.

One day, while they were by a water pump, Anne spelled the word "water" into Helen's hand as the cool water flowed over them. Suddenly, everything changed! Helen realized that the symbols Anne was forming represented real things in her world. It was a breakthrough moment that ignited a fire in her heart! From then on, she eagerly learned more words, eager to bridge the gap between her and the world.

Helen didn't just stop at learning how to communicate. She became a trailblazer, attending Radcliffe College and becoming the first deaf-blind person to earn a Bachelor of Arts degree. But Helen was not just an academic; she was a warrior for change. She traveled the world, sharing her message of hope and empowerment for people with disabilities, showing everyone that their challenges could be transformed into strengths.

So, what can we learn from Helen Keller? Resilience comes from finding new ways to communicate and grow. When faced with obstacles, we can adapt, seek help, and discover new paths to express ourselves. Just like Helen, you have the strength to overcome any challenge life throws your way.

Whenever you encounter tough times, remember Helen's incredible journey. Embrace your curiosity, reach out for support, and believe that even the hardest obstacles can be conquered with determination and creativity. You have the power to turn the impossible into possible!

CHAPTER 13:

Michael Jordan – Bouncing Back from Failure

If you ever think that being the best at something means you never fail, then let me tell you the story of Michael Jordan! Even the greatest basketball player of all time faced setbacks, and his journey shows us that failure can actually help you bounce back stronger than ever.

Once upon a time, in the sunny town of Wilmington, North Carolina, a young Michael was dribbling a basketball and dreaming big. He loved the game and practiced every chance he got. But there was one little problem—when he tried out for his high school basketball team, he didn't make it! Can you believe that? The coach thought he needed more experience, and just like that, Michael was cut from the team. Imagine how disappointed he felt! It was like a thunderstorm rolled into his dreams, leaving him soaked and sad.

But instead of letting that setback define him, Michael decided to turn things around. He went home that day and thought, "If I want to be great, I need to work even harder!" And work hard he did! Michael spent hours practicing his shots, running drills, and building his skills. Every dribble, every jump shot, and every missed basket became a stepping stone toward his goals. He knew that failure was not the end; it was just a part of the journey to success.

As the months passed, Michael's determination and hard work paid off. He tried out for the team again, and this time, he made it! His incredible talent began to shine, and he quickly became a star player. He led his high school team to victory and caught the attention of college scouts everywhere. Eventually, he played for North Carolina and won a national championship, but that was just the beginning of his legendary career.

When Michael was drafted by the Chicago Bulls in 1984, he soared to fame. With his dazzling dunks and impressive skills, he captured the hearts of basketball fans around the world. But it's important to remember that even with all his success, Michael faced more failures and challenges. He was defeated in the playoffs multiple times before finally winning his first championship. Each time he stumbled, he picked himself back up, learned from his mistakes, and came back stronger.

So, what's the lesson we can learn from Michael Jordan? Failure is an opportunity for growth. Instead of fearing failure, we should embrace it as a chance to learn and improve. Just like Michael, when you encounter obstacles, remember that each setback can lead to an even greater comeback.

Whenever you face challenges in sports, school, or anything else, channel your inner Michael Jordan! Use those moments to grow, learn, and bounce back higher than before. With perseverance and a little grit, you, too, can achieve your dreams, no matter how many times you stumble along the way!

CHAPTER 14:

Rosa Parks – Courage in the Face of Injustice

In a world where standing up for what is right can change the course of history, Rosa Parks is a shining example of bravery and courage. Her story is not just about one act of defiance; it's about the power of standing firm in the face of injustice.

It was a chilly December evening in Montgomery, Alabama, in 1955. Rosa was riding home on a crowded bus after a long day of work at a local department store. The bus was filled with people, and as it stopped to pick up more passengers, the driver announced that the black passengers had to give up their seats for white passengers. Rosa, seated in the front row of the "colored" section, was exhausted. She was tired—not just from her day but from years of discrimination and unfair treatment.

When the driver ordered her to give up her seat for a white passenger, something inside Rosa sparked. Instead of moving, she sat still, her heart pounding with both fear and determination. Her refusal to give up her seat was a small act, but it carried enormous weight. It was as if she was saying, "No more! I deserve to be treated with respect!" When the police arrived, they arrested her, but Rosa stood firm. She knew that this was bigger than just one bus ride; it was about standing up against the injustice that African Americans faced every single day.

Rosa's brave decision ignited a powerful movement. The Montgomery Bus Boycott began the very next day. Imagine thousands of people refusing to ride the buses, walking miles to work, or carpooling with friends. It was a display of unity and strength! For more than a year, African Americans in Montgomery stood together, showing the world that they would not accept unfair treatment. They wanted change, and they were willing to fight for it.

Rosa's courage inspired many other activists to join the cause. Leaders like Martin Luther King Jr. rose to prominence during this time, advocating for civil rights through peaceful protests. The boycott was a success, leading to a Supreme Court ruling that declared segregation on public buses unconstitutional. It was a historic victory, and it all started with one woman's brave choice to take a stand.

Rosa Parks became known as the "mother of the civil rights movement." But her journey didn't end there. She continued to fight for justice throughout her life, speaking out for equal rights and inspiring generations to come. She believed that everyone deserved to be treated equally, regardless of their skin color.

So, what can we learn from Rosa Parks? Resilience is standing firm in the face of unfairness. Whenever you witness injustice, remember that you can choose to be brave and stand up for what's right, just like Rosa did. Your voice matters, and your actions can inspire change.

Whenever you feel discouraged or see something unfair happening around you, think of Rosa's courageous heart. She turned her fear into action and helped spark a movement that changed the world. You, too, have the power to make a difference, no matter how small you may feel. Stand tall, be brave, and remember that even the smallest act of courage can lead to incredible change!

CHAPTER 15:

Jessica Meir - Rising Above Hardship

In a world full of challenges, one woman soared to extraordinary heights, both literally and figuratively. Jessica Meir is not just any astronaut; she's a trailblazer who faced adversity with determination and courage, proving that rising above hardship can lead to incredible achievements.

Born in Caribou, Maine, Jessica grew up in a small town where dreams of becoming an astronaut seemed as distant as the stars. From a young age, she was captivated by the mysteries of the universe. But her journey to the stars wasn't easy. Jessica faced obstacles that could have stopped anyone else in their tracks. She loved science, but in a world where fewer girls pursued careers in STEM (science, technology, engineering, and mathematics), she had to work extra hard to follow her passion.

Even after excelling in school and earning her doctorate in marine biology, Jessica faced setbacks. She applied to become an astronaut with NASA multiple times and faced rejection. But instead of giving up, she saw these rejections as opportunities to grow. Each "no" fueled her determination to improve her skills and knowledge.

Finally, her perseverance paid off. In 2013, she was selected as a NASA astronaut! Can you imagine the excitement? Jessica was ready to embark on a journey that would take her far beyond the Earth. In September 2019, she made history when she participated in the first all-female spacewalk, an incredible milestone that inspired countless girls and boys around the world.

But Jessica's journey wasn't just about reaching for the stars. While in space, she conducted important scientific research, studying how microgravity affects the human body. This research not only helps us understand our own health but could also aid astronauts on long missions to Mars and beyond.

What makes Jessica's story even more inspiring is her belief in the importance of education and helping others. She often shares her journey with students, encouraging them to pursue their dreams, no matter the obstacles. She emphasizes that every challenge is a chance to learn and grow and that empathy can be a powerful tool in making the world a better place.

So, what can we learn from Jessica Meir? Overcoming hardship builds resilience and empathy. Just like Jessica, we all face challenges that might make us doubt our abilities. But if we keep pushing forward, learn from our setbacks, and lend a helping hand to others along the way, we can rise above and achieve greatness.

Whenever you encounter difficulties, remember Jessica's journey. With resilience in your heart and a spirit of empathy, you, too, can reach for the stars and inspire others to do the same!

PART FOUR

GROWTH MINDSET iN ACTiON

CHAPTER 16:

Elon Musk – Innovating for the Future

In a world where imagination meets technology, Elon Musk stands out as one of the most daring innovators of our time. With dreams that stretch beyond our planet, Elon has proven that a growth mindset can open doors to incredible possibilities.

Born in Pretoria, South Africa, in 1971, Elon was a curious kid who loved to tinker with electronics and computers. Even as a child, he dreamed of changing the world. After moving to the United States to attend the

University of Pennsylvania, he started diving headfirst into his entrepreneurial spirit. But the journey wasn't easy. He faced many hurdles, including skepticism and failure, yet he never let those challenges dim his vision.

Elon's big dreams began with Zip2, a company he co-founded that helped newspapers create online city guides. After selling it, he didn't stop there. He had a grander vision: to revolutionize transportation on Earth and in space! Enter SpaceX, his ambitious project to make space travel more affordable and eventually allow humans to live on other planets. Sounds like a science fiction movie, right? But for Elon, it was just the beginning.

Launching rockets is no easy feat. SpaceX faced numerous setbacks, including failed rocket launches that would leave many feeling defeated. But not Elon! With each failure, he learned and adapted, pushing his team to innovate and improve. He famously said, "Failure is an option here. If things are not failing, you are not innovating enough." That's a bold mindset!

In 2008, after a series of unsuccessful attempts, SpaceX finally made history by successfully launching the Falcon 1, becoming the first privately funded company to send a rocket to orbit. Can you imagine the celebration? But Elon didn't stop there. He turned his sights to Tesla, determined to change the world of transportation with electric cars. Like SpaceX, Tesla faced its share of obstacles, including production delays and financial troubles. Yet, through resilience and sheer determination, Elon and his team pushed through. Today, Tesla is a leader in sustainable energy and has helped spark a global movement toward electric vehicles.

What's the takeaway from Elon Musk's incredible journey? A growth mindset allows you to push the boundaries of what's possible. When you face challenges, remember that every setback is a chance to learn and grow. Like Elon, don't be afraid to dream big and take risks because sometimes the biggest ideas can change the world.

So, whenever you feel overwhelmed or think your dreams are too big, think of Elon Musk. Let his story inspire you to reach for the stars, embrace challenges, and believe that with perseverance and a growth mindset, you can achieve anything you set your mind to!

I CAN REINVENT MYSELF

CHAPTER 17:

Steve Jobs – Resilience Through Reinvention

In the world of technology, few names resonate like Steve Jobs. Known for his creativity and vision, Steve's journey is a powerful story about resilience and the ability to reinvent oneself in the face of adversity.

Steve was born in San Francisco in 1955 and was a bit of a dreamer from a young age. He loved tinkering with electronics and had a passion for design. In 1976, he co-founded Apple in his parents' garage with his friend

Steve Wozniak. Together, they created the Apple I computer, which set the stage for the future of personal computing. But as Apple grew, so did the challenges.

In the early 1980s, Apple launched the Apple Lisa and the Macintosh, two groundbreaking products that were not only innovative but also changed how people interacted with technology. However, things took a sharp turn when the company faced financial difficulties and internal strife. In a shocking twist, in 1985, Steve Jobs was ousted from the very company he helped create. It was a devastating moment for him—one that could have made anyone give up on their dreams.

But instead of retreating, Steve embraced this unexpected change. He took this opportunity to explore new ventures. He founded NeXT, a computer platform development company, and purchased Pixar, which would go on to create some of the most beloved animated films of all time, including Toy Story. Through these experiences, he learned valuable lessons about creativity, technology, and leadership.

Years later, Apple was struggling to regain its footing. In 1997, after years of competing against Apple, Steve returned to the company he founded. This comeback was nothing short of legendary! With his vision and relentless drive, he began to reinvent Apple from the ground up. He introduced groundbreaking products like the iMac, iPod, and iPhone, turning Apple into one of the most valuable companies in the world.

What can we learn from Steve Jobs' remarkable journey? Resilience means embracing change and reinventing yourself. Life may throw unexpected challenges your way, but how you respond defines your path. Instead of seeing obstacles as setbacks, view them as opportunities to learn and grow.

Whenever you feel discouraged or uncertain about your dreams, think of Steve Jobs. His story reminds us that resilience is about bouncing back, adapting to change, and believing in yourself, no matter how tough things get. With creativity and determination, you, too, can reinvent your journey and achieve greatness!

I FOLLOW MY PASSIONS WITH HEART.

CHAPTER 18:

Jane Goodall - Following Passion and Curiosity

Imagine a world filled with wild animals, dense jungles, and the thrill of discovery. That was the world of Jane Goodall, a remarkable woman who dedicated her life to understanding and protecting our closest relatives in the animal kingdom—chimpanzees.

Born in London in 1934, Jane was a curious child with a deep love for animals. She would spend hours reading about wildlife, dreaming of the day she could explore far-off places.

When she was just 26, she got her big break! With a notebook and a heart full of passion, Jane traveled to Tanzania to study chimpanzees in the wild. But this wasn't just a fun adventure—it was the beginning of a groundbreaking journey that would change our understanding of these incredible creatures forever.

Arriving in Tanzania, Jane faced numerous challenges. Armed with nothing more than her keen observation skills, she spent months watching chimpanzees in their natural habitat. Unlike other scientists of her time, who studied animals from afar, Jane got up close and personal with these amazing primates. She watched them forage for food, socialize, and even use tools—yes, you heard that right! Chimpanzees can make tools, like using sticks to fish for termites. This discovery was revolutionary! It showed that humans weren't the only beings capable of complex behavior.

Despite facing skepticism from the scientific community, Jane's unwavering dedication and passion for her work led her to make groundbreaking contributions to our understanding of animal behavior and conservation. She spent over 60 years in Africa, working tirelessly to protect chimpanzees and their habitats. Through her research and advocacy, she inspired countless people around the globe to care for wildlife and the environment.

So, what can we learn from Jane Goodall's incredible journey? Pursuing what you love leads to lifelong learning and impact. When you follow your passions, as Jane did with her love for animals, you open yourself up to new adventures and knowledge. Her story teaches us that curiosity is a powerful tool— one that can lead to discoveries that change the world.

Whenever you feel unsure about your dreams or interests, remember Jane Goodall. Her life is a reminder that when you follow your heart and embrace your curiosity, you can make a meaningful difference in the world. So go ahead—explore, ask questions, and let your passions guide you on your own incredible journey!

CHAPTER 19:

Maya Angelou – Using Words to Heal

Maya Angelou's life story is like a vibrant tapestry woven from threads of strength, creativity, and resilience. Born in St. Louis in 1928, Maya faced a challenging start when her parents separated, and she was sent with her brother to live with their grandmother in Stamps, Arkansas. Life in Stamps was both comforting and difficult, filled with love from her grandmother but also the harsh realities of racism and poverty.

When Maya was just seven years old, a traumatic event turned her world upside down. After experiencing a terrible incident, she lost her ability to speak, believing her voice had caused the pain around her. For nearly five years, she lived in silence, feeling like a bird trapped in a cage. But instead of letting her silence defeat her, Maya turned to books. She discovered the magic of stories, diving into the works of great authors like Charles Dickens, Shakespeare, and Edgar Allan Poe. Books became her refuge, igniting her imagination and nurturing her spirit.

Finally, after five long years of silence, something changed. A teacher named Mrs. Bertha Flowers encouraged Maya to speak again by introducing her to poetry and literature. She recited poems and learned to express herself through the very words that once felt like chains. The moment Maya spoke again was like the sun breaking through the clouds—her voice was powerful, and her heart was full of stories to share.

As she grew older, Maya transformed her pain into art. She became a dancer, singer, and actress, performing in places around the world. Yet it was her writing that would leave a lasting mark. In 1969, Maya published her groundbreaking autobiography, "I Know Why the Caged Bird Sings." This book was revolutionary; it opened up conversations about race, identity, and the struggles of being a woman. It resonated deeply with readers everywhere, showing them that they could rise above their circumstances.

But Maya didn't stop there. She used her voice as a tool for change, becoming an advocate for civil rights alongside leaders like Martin Luther King Jr. and Malcolm X. Her words inspired countless individuals to fight for justice, equality, and a better world. Maya's poetry, filled with emotion and truth, acted like a healing balm, reminding everyone that they were not alone in their struggles.

What can we learn from Maya Angelou's incredible journey? Self-expression through creativity can lead to personal and societal healing. Maya taught us that our voices matter. By sharing our stories, we can connect with others and foster understanding. Every poem, every story she shared, was a step toward healing—not just for herself but for everyone who read her words.

Whenever you feel like your voice doesn't matter or struggle to express yourself, remember Maya Angelou. Her legacy shines brightly, reminding us that creativity has the power to heal, uplift, and bring about change. So pick up a pen, paintbrush, or any way you can express your unique voice, and let your creativity soar!

I CREATE BEAUTY FROM CHALLENGES

CHAPTER 20:

Beethoven – Composing Through Hardship

Ludwig van Beethoven was not just any composer; he was a musical wizard who changed the world with his extraordinary talent! Born in Bonn, Germany, in 1770, Beethoven showed signs of brilliance early on. By the time he was a child, he was already dazzling audiences with his incredible piano skills and impressive compositions. People said he had music in his bones!

As he grew up, Beethoven quickly became one of the most respected musicians in

Europe. His compositions were beautiful and filled with emotion and depth. But then, in his late twenties, something alarming happened: he began to lose his hearing. At first, it was just a slight ringing in his ears, something he thought would pass. But over the years, it grew worse. Imagine being a pianist, surrounded by melodies and harmonies, but slowly realizing that you can't hear them anymore! It was a scary thought that would terrify anyone.

For many, this would have been a devastating blow. Beethoven was filled with fear and uncertainty. How could he compose music if he couldn't hear it? How could he perform for audiences? Instead of giving up, though, he faced this challenge head-on. Beethoven was made of tougher stuff. He knew he had a passion that couldn't be silenced.

To adapt to his hearing loss, he started to use creative methods. He found that he could feel the vibrations of the piano through his body. He would place a wooden stick against the piano, one end on the instrument and the other against his body, feeling the music pulsing through him. This was how he connected with his music, how he continued to compose, and how he proved that nothing could stop his creativity.

Despite the darkness that threatened to engulf him, Beethoven continued to compose some of his greatest works during this period of silence. One of his most famous pieces, the Ninth Symphony, was composed when he was almost completely deaf. This incredible work features the legendary "Ode to Joy," a powerful anthem of hope and unity that celebrates the joys of life. The symphony was not just a musical achievement; it was a triumphant declaration that music could transcend all barriers, even the barrier of sound itself. Imagine a crowd of thousands, filled with joy and excitement, all singing together, united by Beethoven's music!

Beethoven's life was a testament to the power of resilience. He believed in the power of music to heal and connect people. His determination to continue composing, even when the world around him grew quieter, taught everyone a valuable lesson:

Even in difficult times, you can continue to create and inspire. Beethoven showed us that hardships can fuel creativity rather than stifle it. He transformed his pain into beauty, proving that challenges can lead to remarkable achievements.

As Beethoven navigated through his struggles, he learned to redefine success on his own terms. He became a symbol of courage for aspiring musicians everywhere. His music inspires people even today, reminding us that our passions can guide us through the toughest challenges.

Whenever you face your own struggles, remember Beethoven's journey. Let his resilience inspire you to keep going, to keep creating, and to let your voice shine brightly, no matter what obstacles come your way. You have the power to create your own symphony, just like Beethoven!

EMILY LYLANI

CONCLUSION

As we reach the end of this book, think about all the incredible people we've met along the way. Inventors, artists, athletes, and leaders—all of them faced tough challenges and made mistakes, just like we all do. But they didn't give up. They learned from their stumbles, turned setbacks into comebacks, and kept moving forward with courage and curiosity.

The same spirit that helped them grow lives inside you, too! Every time you tackle something new, keep trying after a mistake, or find a way to help others, you're building a stronger, braver version of yourself. This is the heart of a growth mindset—the belief that with practice, you can learn and improve at anything. And that's exactly how you can achieve amazing things, just like the people in these stories.

Now, the world is waiting for your story! Use what you've learned from these inspiring lives to take on your own challenges, follow your curiosity, and dream big. Keep learning, keep exploring, and don't forget—every small step counts. Whether it's inventing something new, helping a friend, or standing up for what's right, each choice you make brings you closer to your best self.

So, as you close this book, remember: this isn't the end of the journey; it's only the beginning. Embrace every challenge, celebrate each victory, and let your curiosity lead the way. Who knows? Maybe someday, someone will be reading your story and feeling just as inspired!

Note from the Author

Dear Reader,

Thank you for joining me on this incredible journey. I hope you enjoyed the stories and learned something new along the way. Your feedback is incredibly valuable to me, and I would love to hear your thoughts.

If you enjoyed the book, please consider leaving a review on the Amazon page. Your review helps me improve and continue creating content that inspires and educates young minds.

Thank you for your support!

Best regards,

Made in United States
North Haven, CT
22 July 2025

70943190R00078